No Allium

Thank You

Joy Thomas

ISBN 978-0-9957408-5-3

Recipes

FOREWARD

Allium – the latin word for garlic

Everyone is different and their reactions to certain foods will be different. For me personally the main no go area is anything from the Allium family: onion (any kind), shallots, leeks, scallions, chives and garlic. They all contain a sulphur compound called allicin, which is primarily responsible for the heat and pungency of the plants.

Absolutely no mustard, Worcester sauce, tinned soups (except some tomato), mayonnaise and some salad creams.

I do find however I am able to eat some sauces or foods that contain just a little onion powder i.e. spaghetti in tomato sauce and baked beans. I can only assume the tomato sauce dilutes the onion powder to such an extent as to make it possible for me to manage. I use my own stock for soups but certain chicken stock cubes do not include any onion powder or garlic.

What irritates me more than anything else is when I ask for a cheese sandwich – just plain cheese – and it arrives with slices of raw onion decorating it or a jacket potato with side salad, likewise decorated with raw onion and possibly coleslaw. It is not something you can just pick off and remove, nor can you use the same knife on my salad after cutting up onion. The taste and smell are too strong.

Please, please, please could caterers stop doing this. If you must use onions and dressings make sure the customer would like it. Do not assume everyone is a lover of the Allium family.

I am not a chef, I have no training in culinary matters, just a housewife with a sensitivity to the above ingredients and have therefore had to adjust recipes and make up my own along the way. I use a great variety of dried herbs, celery for soups and stews, green peppers and fruit, usually mango, but also sultanas and apple. Honey is a good addition too if you need a little extra sweetness, and I absolutely rely on the sweet potato – it's a life saver.

This book is dedicated to all those people, who like me, struggle to eat out or buy sandwiches which do not contain any additives we cannot tolerate.

PRODUCTS I FIND I CAN SAFELY EAT

(even baked beans usually contain onion powder)

(Bear in mind manufacturers can change ingredients from time to time – always check labels)

- Young's Frozen Gastro Signature Breaded Lemon & Pepper Fish fillets. (Alaska Pollock)
- Marmite
- Most cans of cream of tomato soup.
- Heinz Cream of Tomato Cup Soup is fine.
- Chicken Oxo (beef oxo contains onion powder)
- Finest Pork Sausages
- Most tinned fish in either oil or brine, the same applies to canned vegetables.
- Original HP Sauce (Tomato Ketchup will usually contain onion and garlic powder).
- Tesco Quiche Lorraine with Beechwood smoked bacon.

SOUPS

Tomato and Fresh Basil Soup

Serves: 4-6

Ingredients

1 tbsp olive oil
2 tbsp butter
900g Italian plum tomatoes, chopped
750ml chicken or vegetable stock
120ml dry white wine
2tbsp tomato purèe
2tbsp chopped fresh basil (or use dried)
150ml double cream
Season with Salt and pepper to taste

Directions

Heat oil and butter in saucepan. Stir in chopped tomatoes and add the stock, white wine and purèe.

Add salt and pepper. Bring to the boil then reduce heat. Half cover the pan and simmer gently for around 20 minutes. Stir occasionally to avoid sticking.

Put soup and basil in blender. Turn out into clean pan adding the double cream. Heat through, stirring. Do not allow to boil. Check for seasoning and consistency before serving in warmed bowls garnished with basil leaves.

Farmhouse Soup

Serves: 4

Ingredients

2 tbsp olive oil
3 carrots
200g turnips
175g swede
400g canned tomato
1 tbsp tomato puree
1 tsp dried mixed herbs
1 tsp oregano
50g peppers
1.5 litre vegetable stock or water
50g small macaroni
400g can red kidney beans
2 tbsp chopped parsley
Salt and pepper to taste

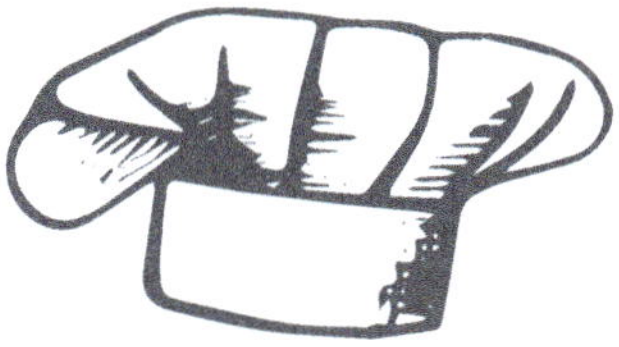

Directions

Heat oil and add fresh vegetables, canned tomato, tomato puree, dried herbs and peppers and cook over low heat. Stir in salt and pepper to taste.

Pour in stock/water. Bring to boil, cover and simmer for 30 min. stirring occasionally.

Add pasta. Stir frequently. Stir in beans for about 3 mins. Add parsley. Taste and adjust as required.

Cream of Avocado

Serves: 4

Ingredients

2 large ripe avocado
1 ltr chicken stock
250ml single cream
Salt and pepper
15ml chopped coriander to garnish (optional)

Directions

Cut avocado in half, remove stone and mash. Put into a sieve and press through into warm bowl. Heat chicken stock with cream in saucepan. When mixture is hot (do not allow to boil), whisk into the purèed avocado. Season to taste. Sprinkle with coriander.

May be served chilled if preferred.

Winter Vegetable

Serves: 8

Ingredients

1.5 ltr stock
1 medium savoy cabbage (sliced)
2 tblsp oil
4 carrots finely sliced
2 celery stalks finely sliced
1 small swede chopped
2 medium potatoes
1 Pepper finely sliced
1 tin chopped tomatoes
1 small sweet potato diced
1 courgette
Herbs to taste
Salt and pepper (about half a tsp each)

Directions

Use a large saucepan and place the cabbage, carrots, celery and swede in the heated oil for about 15 minutes, stirring frequently. Stir in stock, add remaining ingredients and bring to the boil. Simmer for about 20-30 minutes until the vegetables are tender. If you prefer a smoother soup you can blend once cooled.

CHICKEN DISHES

Chicken and Mushroom Hotpot

Serves: 4

Ingredients

2 tbsp oil
8 chicken joints approx.. 1.25kg
25g flour
1 can condensed cream of mushroom soup (please check ingredients, some have onion and/or garlic)
300ml chicken stock or white wine
100g baby carrots
Coriander, salt and pepper to taste

Directions

Preheat oven. Heat oil in flameproof casserole dish. Toss the chicken pieces in flour and fry for 10 mins, turning until browned on all sides.

Add soup and stock or wine, stirring well.

Bring to the boil to thicken.

(If needed I sometimes add chicken granules as I can tolerate these).

Stir in carrots and some chopped coriander, season to taste.

Cover and cook for 1-1.5 hours or until the chicken is tender and cooked through.

You can also add some chopped bacon with the carrots for extra flavour.

Pesto Chicken Burgers

Serves: 4

Ingredients

750g sweet potatoes cut into wedges
1 tbsp olive oil
4 breaded chicken steaks
250g mozzarella, drained and sliced into 4
4 soft wholemeal rolls
4 tbsp basil pesto (see Index for recipe)
30g rocket leaves

Directions

Preheat oven to 200c/fan 180/gas 6

Put sweet potato wedges onto baking tray season and toss with the oil to coat. Roast on top shelf for 30-35 mins. turning halfway.

Put chicken steaks on separate tray and bake on the shelf beneath the wedges for 25 mins or until crisp. Top with mozzarella slices and bake for 5 mins more until the cheese has melted.

Half and toast the rolls. Spread half the pesto onto bases.

Add the chicken and top with remaining pesto and rocket.

Sandwich with the tops of the buns and serve alongside the sweet potato wedges.

Sweet and Sour Chicken

Serves: 4

Ingredients

2 small carrots thinly sliced
1 green pepper cut into strips
4 level tbls. Canned pineapple
4 tbls. Juice from pineapple
1 tbls. Soy sauce (if you can tolerate)
1 tbls. Clear honey
25gm soft brown sugar
4 tbls. vinegar
2 level tbls. Cornflower
250ml chicken stock
25grams blanched almonds
25 grams butter
2 kilo chicken cut into cubes once cooked.
Salt and pepper to taste.

Directions

Put carrots, pepper, pineapple, honey, sugar, vinegar and soy sauce into pan.

Bring to boil and simmer for 5 min.

Blend cornflower and stock to smooth cream.

Add to pan. Stir until sauce thickens then add salt and pepper, almonds and butter. Leave over a very low heat until ready.

Pour over chicken pieces.

Chicken and Walnuts

Ingredients

6 Chicken joints
2 tbsp sherry
2 tbsp caster sugar
3 tbsp olive oil
225g mushrooms
175g water chestnuts
1 pint (570ml) chicken stock
2 tbsp cornflour
110g walnuts
75g butter

Directions

Pour sherry and caster sugar over chicken and leave to marinate for 1-2 hours. Heat oil in frying pan and brown chicken pieces. Slice mushrooms, drain and dice chestnuts and put all together in casserole. Place chicken on top, pour stock and juices over and bake in oven at 180C/gas 4 for 2 hours.

Drain off liquor, keep hot and thicken with cornflour.

Brown walnuts in melted butter for 4-5 minutes and drain.

FISH DISHES

Salmon with Mint, Strawberry & Melon Salsa

Serves: 4

Ingredients

1 tsp coriander seeds
200g strawberries, hulled and chopped
175g cantaloupe melon, peeled and deseeded
1 lemon, zested, plus 2tbsp juice
30g fresh mint, leaves finely chopped
1tbsp olive oil
2 boneless salmon steaks

Directions

Preheat oven to 180/fan 160/gas 4

To make salsa, toast the coriander seeds in a dry frying pan over a medium heat for 2 minutes, shaking pan occasionally. Crush roughly and tip into mixing bowl with the strawberries, melon, lemon zest and juice, mint and 1tbsp oil. Season to taste and set aside.

Place salmon steaks on foil and drizzle with oil, Cover and bake in oven for 10 minutes, open foil and cook for a further 10 minutes. or until firm and cooked through.

Serve with prepared salsa.

Salmon Plait

Serves: 4

Ingredients

6-8 tbsp left over rice
200g tin salmon
350g cheese sauce mix and 1 tbsp grated parmesan
1 bag watercress, chopped
1 box Jus-rol's frozen Already Rolled Puff Pastry sheet

Directions

Mix together rice, salmon, cheese sauce and watercress; season well.

Unroll the pastry into an oblong, pile the cold mix in a line down the middle.

Cut pastry sides into diagonal strips and fold over alternately to make a plait on top of the salmon mix. Brush with milk or beaten egg and bake for 30 minutes 200c/ gas 6. Serve with bowl of mixed salad leaves.

Trout with Mint and Orange

Serves: 4 Oven 160C/gas mark 3 | Cooking Time: about 45-50 minutes

Ingredients

4 rainbow trout, cleaned
50g butter
Finely grated rind of ½ orange
2 tbsp orange juice
2 tbsp dry vermouth
1 tbsp finely chopped fresh mint (or 1 teaspoon dried mint flakes)

For the stuffing:
75g fresh brown breadcrumbs
50g button mushrooms, chopped
1 tbsp finely chopped fresh mint or mint flakes
Finely grated rind of ½ an orange
Salt and pepper to taste
2-3 tbsp orange juice.

Directions

Prepare the stuffing, mixing together the breadcrumbs, mushrooms, mint and orange rind. Season well and bind together with orange juice. Divide into four and use to stuff the trout.

Arrange trout close together in a lightly greased, shallow casserole. Heat the butter in a pan until it just starts to brown then stir in orange rind, orange juice, vermouth and mint. Pour over the trout.

Cover the casserole and cook in preheated oven for about 35 minutes. Remove the cover, spoon a little of the sauce over the trout and return, uncovered, to the oven for a further 10 minutes or until cooked through.

Serve garnished with orange slices and springs of mint.

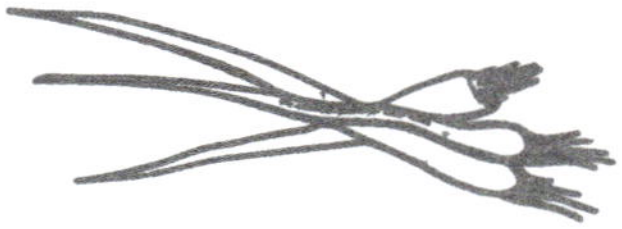

Tuna and Pasta Bake

Ingredients

600g pasta
2 x 160g cans tuna,drained

For sauce:
50g butter, 50g plain flour, 600ml milk,
250g strong cheddar.
Sweetcorn/peas can be added if required
Chopped parsley.

Directions

Heat oven to 180C/gas 4

Boil pasta for 5 min.

Make sauce:

Melt butter in pan and stir in plain flour for
1 min. then gradually stir in milk until smooth.
Remove from heat and stir all but a handful of cheddar.
Drain pasta and mix with sauce. Add tuna, season as required with parsley.
Place in baking dish and top with remaining cheese.
Bake until cheese topping is starting to brown – approx.. 15-20 min

EGG DISHES

Eggy Bread

Serves: 2

Ingredients

1 large egg
4 tbsp milk or single cream
2 slices thick bread
30g butter

Directions

Break egg into a shallow bowl and whisk well.

Stir in milk.

Dip bread into the egg mixture and coat both sides well.

Heat half of the butter in a frying pan and gently fry eggy bread for about 1 minute on each side or until golden brown and crispy.
Take care not to let it burn.

Serve immediately.

Egg and Bacon Pie

Serves: 4-6

Ingredients

For pastry:

100g g butter
200g plain flour
1-2 tbsp cold water

For filling:

15g butter
4 lean streaky bacon rashers, diced
55g cheddar cheese, grated
2 eggs, beaten
300ml single cream
Pepper to taste.

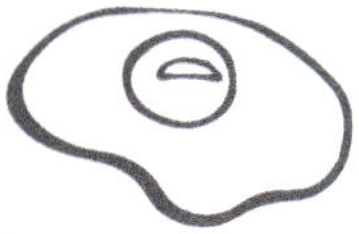

Directions

For pastry:

Rub butter and flour with fingertips until mixture resembles fine breadcrumbs. Stir in just enough water to bind to a firm dough. Roll out on a lightly floured surface and use to line a 23cm loose based round pie tin. Prick the base with a fork. Chill for at least 10 minutes.

Pre heat oven to 200C/gas 6. Line pastry case with baking paper and beans, place on a baking tray and bake for 10 minutes. Remove paper and beans and bake for a further 10 minutes.

For filling:

Melt butter in pan and cook bacon for about 5 minutes. Spread in pastry case and sprinkle with half the cheese. Beat together the eggs and cream and season with pepper.

Pour into the pastry case and sprinkle with the remaining cheese.

Reduce oven tempertautre to 190C/gas 5. Bake for 25-30 minutes or until golden brown and just set.

Cool for 10 minutes before turning out.

For easier make – use ready to roll pastry.

Baked Eggs with Cream, Spinach & Parmesan

Ingredients

2 tbsp butter
125g spinach
½ tsp grated nutmeg
4 eggs
4tbsp single cream
2 tbsp grated Parmesan cheese
Season to taste

Directions

Preheat oven to 160C/gas 3.

Lightly grease 2 small individual dishes

Melt butter in pan over low heat and add spinach. Cook for 1 minute stirring with a wooden spoon until the spinach starts to wilt. Season with a little nutmeg then divide between the prepared dishes.

Gently break 2 eggs into each dish. Pour cream over and sprinkle with grated Parmesan. Season to taste. Bake in preheated oven for 10 minutes or until the whites of the eggs have set but the yolks remain runny.

Serve immediately

Savoury Omelette

Surely the most versatile of dishes and one available wherever you travel.

Ingredients

2/3 free range eggs
Salt and pepper to season
A dash of water or milk

Directions

Whisk eggs, add water/milk and season.

Heat a little oil in pan and once hot pour in egg mixture. Add filling and fold.

Possible fillings:

Mushrooms
Cheese
Tomato
Mixed vegetables

Eat immediately.

BEEF

Steak with Port and Peaches

Serves: 4

Ingredients

200g button mushrooms
62g butter
1 large can peach halves (1 kilo)
4 rump or fillet steaks (approx. 150g)
6 tbsp port
4 slices of bread, fried in butter and kept hot
1 tbsp double cream
Season to taste and garnish with parsley

Directions

Brown the mushrooms quickly in half the butter and season to taste.

Heat peaches in their own juice, strain and keep warm.

Melt remaining butter and brown steaks on both sides. Remove from pan and keep warm.

Add port to juices in pan and bring to boil.

Replace steaks, add mushrooms and drained peaches and simmer for 5 minutes.

Serve steaks on slices of fried bread, garnish with peaches and mushrooms.

Add cream to sauce and bring to the boil.

Cover each steak, decorate with parsley.

Corned Beef Alaska

Serves: 4

Ingredients

1 300g can corned beef
1 tbsp tomato puree
¾ kilo freshly boiled potatoes
25g butter or margarine
Hot milk
25g finely grated Cheddar cheese
Season to taste.

Directions

Pre-heat oven to 200C/gas 6

Stand corned beef on a greased heatproof plate, spread with tomato puree.

Mash potatoes finely, beat to a light cream with butter and hot milk.

Season to taste and pile over corned beef.

Sprinkle with cheese and bake just above centre of oven for 30 minutes or until brown and heated through.

Serve immediately.

Cottage Pie

Serves: 4

Ingredients

25 grams butter
½ kilo minced beef
1 level tablespoon flour
125ml beef stock or water (check for onion in the beef stock cube)
1 desert spoon HP sauce (or any brown sauce without onion and garlic)
Salt and pepper to season
¾ kilo freshly boiled potatoes
37 grams butter for mashed potatoes
2 tablespoons hot milk
25 grams grated cheese

Directions

Pre-heat oven to 180°/gas 4
Heat butter in pan and add meat until lightly brown, breaking it up with a fork.
Stir in flour and blend in stock and brown sauce.
Bring to boil and simmer for 5 minutes, stirring. Season with salt and pepper.
Transfer to a greased dish (approximately 2" deep)
Mash previously boiled potatoes with butter and milk.
Fork over to completely cover mince and sprinkle with grated cheese.
Cook in oven for 30 minutes.

PORK

Gammon and Pineapple

Serves: 4

Ingredients

4 gammon steaks each approximately 150g each in weight.
Melted butter.
Can of pineapple rings/fresh pineapple to top each steak.

Directions

Remove rinds from gammon steaks then snip fat at close intervals round each steak to prevent curling as it cooks.

Brush with melted butter and place under pre-heated grill.

Grill for 7 minutes then turn.

Brush with more butter and continue to grill for a further 7 minutes or until gammon is cooked through.

Serve steaks with rings or alternatively, as a change, with fried canned peach halves or fried banana halves.

Italian Pasta Bake

Serves: 4

Ingredients

225g penne pasta
Salt and pepper
275g ham, cut into pieces
Butter for greasing oven proof dish
3 eggs
450ml single cream
150g mature cheese, grated
50g parmesan cheese

Directions

Preheat oven to 190C/375F/gas 5.

Put pasta in a pan of boiling salted water and cook for 8-10 mins. Until just tender. Drain well.

Stir ham into pasta and put into greased ovenproof dish.

Beat together the eggs, cream and seasoning and add half the cheese. Pour over pasta.

Sprinkle remaining mature and parmesan cheese over the top and bake for 40mins until golden brown.

Sausage and Apple Tray Bake

Serves: 4

Ingredients

8 pork sausages
4 medium baking potatoes, unpeeled and chopped in to wedges.
4 apples, cored and sliced
1 tbsp honey
Fresh thyme (approx.. 6 sprigs)

Directions

Pre-heat oven to 210C/190C fan gas 8

In large roasting tin toss the sausages, potatoes and apple wedges in a little oil and season with salt and pepper.

Roast for 40 minutes adding the thyme after the first 20 minutes, turning everything over at the same time.

Once the sausages, potatoes and apples are golden and caramelised, remove from oven and drizzle with the honey.

Serve immediately.

LAMB

Lamb Rosettes

Serves: 2-3

Ingredients

½ kilo potatoes
1 red pepper
2 medium celery stalks
2 medium carrots
125ml dry cider
Salt and pepper to taste
1 large lamb breast, boned, rolled and tied
Parsley to garnish

Directions

Pre-heat oven to 200C/gas 6

Slice potatoes fairly thickly.

Halve red pepper, remove seeds and cut flesh into thin strips.

Cut celery into diagonal slices and each carrot lengthwise into 4 long strips.

Put vegetables into roasting tin, add cider then sprinkle with salt and pepper to taste.

Place lamb on top and cover with foil.

Roast in centre of oven for 1 hour.

Arrange vegetable in a warm dish.

Cut lamb into slices and place on top of vegetables.

Garnish with parsley and serve.

Lamb Cutlets with Apricots

Serves: 4

Ingredients

50g butter
2 level tsp rosemary
8 lamb cutlets
Salt and pepper
200g dried apricots, soaked overnight, drained and chopped
50g sultanas, soaked overnight, drained and chopped
Juice of ½ lemon
1 can-200g- apricot halves, drained
4oz cottage cheese

Directions

Beat butter and rosemary well together and spread over each cutlet.
Season as required
Grill cutlets for 3/4 minutes each side.
Meanwhile place dried apricots, sultanas and lemon juice into saucepan.
Simmer 2/3 minutes, top each cutlet with mix.
Garnish with canned apricot halves filled with cottage cheese and serve.

Roasted Lamb Shoulder

Serves: 4

Ingredients

½ lamb shoulder, boned or de-boned
4 sprigs of rosemary
4 sprigs of thyme
2 sprigs of mint
1 carrot, chopped
3 celery sticks, chopped
1 tbsp olive oil
Salt and pepper

For the Gravy:

200ml chicken stock
25ml port
Salt and pepper

Directions

Lamb should be at room temperature. Cut the fat side of the lamb, rub with salt and black pepper all over. Heat the oven to its maximum temperature. In a large pot heat up the olive oil. Brown the lamb shoulder all over to seal the meat.

Place all the chopped vegetables in a baking tray, put two sprigs of rosemary, thyme and mint on top of the vegetables. Transfer the lamb to the baking tray and lay the rest of the rosemary and thyme on top. Cover the top of the baking tray tightly with foil. Reduce oven heat to 170C and roast for 3 hours.

For the gravy:

Add chicken stock and port into the baking tray, heat the tray on the hob. Add the vegetables and bring to boil, let it simmer to reduce the sauce.

When ready, sieve the gravy and serve with new potatoes and vegetables of choice.

SALADS

Lemon Chicken Salad

Serves: 4

Ingredients

Mixed green salad i.e little gem, lollo bionde, frisee
4 boneless, skinless chicken breasts
5 rashers of rindless back bacon
Salt and pepper to season
1 tablespoon freshly chopped tarragon
Olive oil
Juice of 1 lemon

Dressing

1 dessertspoon olive oil
1 tablespoon vinegar
lemon juice
a sprinkle of oregano.

Directions

Prepare green salad

Slice chicken breasts into strips and chop the bacon into small pieces.

Heat some oil in saucepan, add chicken and bacon and cook for 4-5 minutes until lightly browned.

Add the lemon juice and tarragon and season to taste.

Cook for a further 4-5 minutes until chicken is tender.

Toss the green salad lightly with dressing and add the chicken and bacon.

Serve Immediately

Salad Flamingo

Serves: 4

Ingredients

1 hard boiled egg
50g cheddar cheese
2 large eating apples
Lemon juice
4 large bananas
2 large tomatoes, skinned and sliced
Salad cream to accompany

Directions

Slice hard boiled egg

Grate cheese

Peel and core apples and cut into slices and arrange on flat serving dish, sprinkle with lemon juice.

Slice bananas and stand them on top of apples. Sprinkle with lemon juice.

Garnish with egg and tomato slices and sprinkle with cheese.

Accompany with salad cream. (be aware this usually contains some mustard powder, check ingredients)

Serve with rice or pasta for a delicious meal.

Oriental salad

Serves: 4

Ingredients

1 medium lettuce
3 celery stalks
300g freshly cooked long grain rice (150g raw)
200 – 300g cold cooked chicken cut into strips.
1 can mandarins, drained.
50g flaked almonds, toasted.
Yogurt dressing. (see below)
3 level tbsp chopped canned pimiento

Yogurt dressing:

1 carton natural yogurt (125ml)
2 tbsp single cream
1 desserts spoon fresh lemon juice
1 level teaspoon caster sugar
Salt and pepper to taste.

Basic French Dressing

4 tbsp olive or salad oil
¼ to ½ teaspoon salt
Pepper to taste
¼ level teaspoon caster sugar
2 tbsp wine or cider vinegar
(or half vinegar and half lemon juice)

Directions

Wash lettuce and shake dry.

Line salad bowl.

Chop celery finely and put into large bowl.

Add rice, chicken, half the drained mandarins and the almonds.

Add dressing and toss gently to combine.

Pile on top of lettuce then garnish with remaining drained mandarins and the pimiento.

Serve immediately.

Italian dressing

Great dressing for accompanying Italian style dishes.

Make up as for basic French dressing, then add 2 level tbsp grated Parmesan cheese at the end.

MISCELLANEOUS

Cauliflower Cheese

Serves: 4

Ingredients

1 medium cauliflower
25g butter
25g flour
125ml milk
125g cheddar cheese, grated
Season to taste

Directions

Cook cauliflower in boiling water until tender.
Drain and reserve 125ml cauliflower water.
Keep cauliflower hot.
Melt butter in saucepan and add flour. Cook for 2 minutes without browning.
Gradually blend in cauliflower water and milk.
Sir continuously until sauce comes to the boil and thickens.
Stir in cheese, leaving a little to use later, and add seasoning.
Transfer to buttered heat proof dish.
Coat with sauce and sprinkle with remaining cheese.
Brown under a hot grill and serve.

Macaroni Cheese

Serves: 4

Ingredients

159g macaroni
37g butter
25g flour
250ml milk
150g cheddar cheese – grated
Pinch of Cayenne pepper
Salt to taste
1 level tbsp toasted breadcrumbs

Directions

Cook macaroni in plenty of boiling salted water until tender (10-15 minutes)
Drain, reserving 250ml water.
Melt 25g butter in saucepan.
Stir in flour and cook for 2 minutes without browning.
Gradually blend in macaroni water and milk.
Stir continuously until sauce comes to boil and thickens.
Simmer for 2 minutes.
Stir in 100g cheese, pepper, salt and macaroni.
Mix thoroughly then transfer to a buttered heatproof dish.
Sprinkle remaining cheese, butter and breadcrumbs over the top.
Brown under a hot grill and serve.

Stuffed Mushrooms

Ingredients

454grams button mushrooms (choose decent size caps)
125grams (1 cup) grated cheese
A little extra virgin olive oil (teaspoon)
1 red pepper,deseeded and finely chopped.
1 teaspoon oregano
1 teaspoon ginger
Pinch of salt and pepper to season
½ cup chopped tomatoes
¼ spoon turmeric
Zest of 1 lemon

Directions

Preheat oven to 220C/gas 7

Remove the stem and lightly scoop out some flesh from the middle.

Put stems and flesh removed from mushrooms on a board and chop into small pieces.

Put cheese, lemon zest, pepper and a little salt and pepper into a bowl and mix with a wooden spoon. Fold in the oregano, ginger and turmeric. Add chopped stems and flesh.

Toss the caps in a little oil with salt and pepper.

Lay on a baking tray and carefully spoon in the filling. Sprinkle a little cheese over the top and bake in the preheated oven till golden – approximately 15 minutes.

Serve immediately on a large platter with a little salad.

Potato Scones

This mixture makes between 12/14 scones

Ingredients

200grams self-raising flour
2 level teaspoons salt
300grams freshly boiled potatoes
50grams butter
Cold milk if necessary

Directions

Pre-heat oven to 200C/gas 7

Sift flour and salt into bowl.

Mash potatoes adding butter.

Gradually add sifted flour using a little milk if mixture is too dry to hold together.

Knead lightly on a floured surface until smooth.

Roll out to ½" thickness and cut into 12/14 rounds.

Transfer to a greased baking tray and bake near the top of the oven for 15 minutes or until well-risen and golden.

Remove from oven, spread tops with butter and serve.

Baked Potatoes with Ricotta and Roasted Tomatoes.

Serves: 4

Ingredients

4 180g baking potatoes
320g cherry tomatoes
2 sprigs of fresh thyme
75g ricotta
1 ½ tsps balsamic vinegar
Cooking oil

Directions

Pre-heat oven to 200C/fan180/gas 6.

Prick potatoes and place on baking tray.

Drizzle with a little olive oil.

Bake for approximately 1 hour 20 minutes or until tender.

Meanwhile put tomatoes and thyme in a small baking dish and drizzle over oil and balsamic vinegar. Season to taste and toss to coat. Bake with potatoes for the final 35 minutes of cooking time.

Remove potatoes and tomatoes from the oven, discarding the thyme. Split the potatoes and top with ricotta and roasted tomatoes.

Season to taste and serve.

Grilled Apricots, with Yogurt, Honey and Pistachios

Ingredients

1 medium can of apricot halves (approx.. 400 grams)
1 large carton Greek yogurt (approx. 500 grams)
1-2 tbls honey
1-2 tbls of chopped pistachio

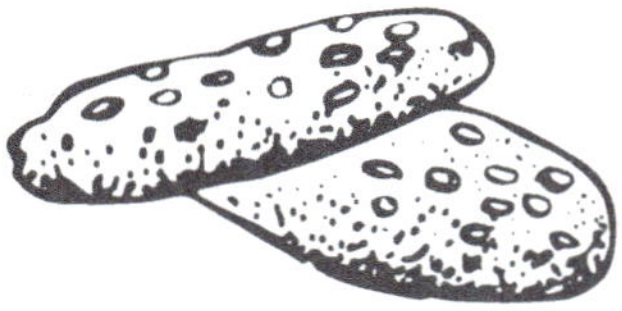

Directions

Using the hob and a nonstick grill pan, grill the flat side of each apricot on medium heat till grill marks appear. Remove from heat and let cool.

Layer yogurt, apricots, honey and pistachio and enjoy!

STUFFING

Prune and Port

A sumptuous stuffing for poultry.

Ingredients

100 grams prunes
1 glass dry white wine
150 grams lean pork, finely minced
1 egg yolk
1 tbsp brandy
1 level tbsp finely chopped parsley
½ level tsp sage (optional)
1 dozen toasted almonds, coarsely chopped
Salt and pepper to taste

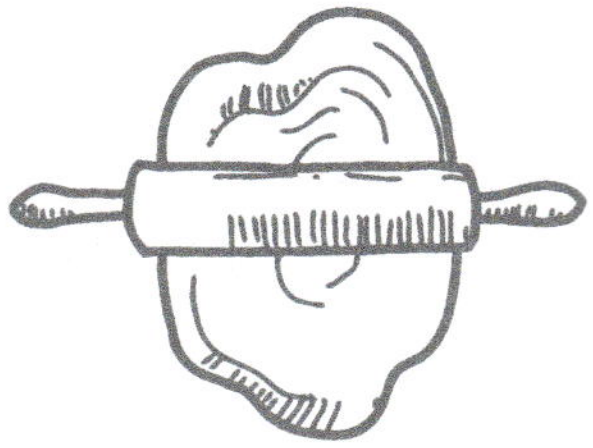

Directions

Soak prunes overnight.

Remove stones and chop finely

Combine with port and all other ingredients to make stuffing mixture.

Parsley, Lemon and Thyme

Ideal for veal, poultry or fish

Ingredients

100 grams white breadcrumbs
25 grams finely shredded suet
1 level tbsp chopped parsley
Grated peel of ½ small lemon
½ level tsp thyme
Salt and pepper to taste
1 standard egg, beaten
Milk or stock if necessary

Directions

Combine crumbs with suet, parsley, lemon peel, thyme and salt and pepper to taste. Bind with beaten egg, adding milk or stock only if necessary.

Apple, Cranberry and Orange

Ingredients

2 large cooking apples
1 200-gram tin of cranberry sauce
1 level tsp finely grated orange peel

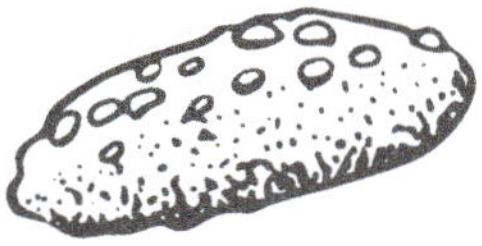

Directions

Peel, core and chop apples.

Combine with cranberry sauce and orange peel

Form mixture into savoury balls.

Just for fun, a poem I wrote several years ago in desperation after standing in a queue waiting to be served.

Garlic

(poem)

I opened the tin and it hit me.
I didn't feel terribly well.
I felt myself wretch as I pushed it away
That vile pungent garlicky smell.

The label just said a bean salad.
How was a person to tell
Hidden inside with no warning
That vile pungent garlicky smell.

I'm sick of continually saying
I only want what keeps me well.
No extra garnish, no onion,
No vile pungent garlicky smell.

Are you aware when I give you a stare
How sick you are making me feel?
On the breath, through the skin,
You ooze like that tin
Of the vile pungent garlicky smell.

When you wait in a queue,
They stand next to you
Wreaking of last nights delight.
If you've had garlic for tea,
Don't sidle to me
With your vile pungent garlicky smell.

Personal Notes and Recipes

Personal Notes and Recipes

Personal Notes and Recipes

Personal Notes and Recipes

Personal Notes and Recipes

Personal Notes and Recipes

Personal Notes and Recipes

Personal Notes and Recipes

Personal Notes and Recipes

Personal Notes and Recipes

Personal Notes and Recipes

Personal Notes and Recipes

Personal Notes and Recipes

JOY THOMAS - BIOGRAPHY

Born in 1944, I lived in St Annes on Sea, Lancashire until moving with my parents to Mufulira, Northern Rhodesia.
We returned to England in 1959 settling in Gloucestershire where I married in 1963. I have three children, three stepchildren, grandchildren and great grandchildren plus a border collie called Bonnie.
I realized at a very young age my intolerance to anything from the Allium family and the difficulties it can produce when eating out. However, there are many alternatives for tasty dishes, and actually eating foods without onions and garlic highlights other flavours often masked by the full bodied alliums.

Previous Publications:

Slipped Through The Net.

Asperger's, Autism and all that Jazz.

When my son was born it was initially denied there was a problem but he was eventually diagnosed with a learning disability, then later in life with Asperger's Syndrome.
Many of the poems in this book were inspired by and written as part of our journey over the last 50 years.

The Syncopation of Life

In this second book I have tried to widen the scope and subjects to envelope a greater variety. As the cover suggests, life is always full of the unexpected and off beat. I hope what I have written will give the reader much pleasure and at the same time, food for thought.

Take Five is my third book exploring feelings, observing behaviour, and hopefully adding a little humour here and there through poetry and short stories. It is my effort to encourage you to stop, if only for five minutes, and escape from the hum drum, constant movement and pressure of everyday life.
We have only one chance. Life is not repeated so make each day matter, be kind to yourself and to each other.

From Rough Towels to Milkshakes

This book is a record of just some of the journey with my son Phillip and his siblings. I decided to write down our experiences, initially in poetry, after hearing the words “slipped through the net” used in a news bulletin. The same words I had personally heard many years ago, along with the phrase “we have learnt lessons”.

For contact information:

joypm@outlook.com
facebook: joy Thomas
www.facebook.com/artbyjoysandwiththomas

Printed in Dunstable, United Kingdom

74220245R00045